I0828195

THIS BOOK BELONGS TO:

WELCOME TO
NEW HAMPSHIRE

SEAL OF THE STATE OF NEW HAMPSHIRE
1776

Dedicated to all the explorers.

ISBN 978-1-958985-85-4

www.joeysavestheday.com

A Mimi Book

New Hampshire was named after Hampshire, a county in southern England. Early English settlers chose the name to honor the place they came from, so they called the new land "New Hampshire." It was their way of bringing a little piece of home across the ocean.

← **NEW HAMPSHIRE**

ENGLAND

A castle in Hampshire, England.

New Hampshire is one of the original 13 colonies and has a long history that began with Native American groups such as the Abenaki. English settlers arrived in the early 1600s, and New Hampshire became its own colony in 1679. It played an important role in the American Revolution and was the first state to create its own constitution in 1776. New Hampshire became a state in 1788 and is known for its early leadership in American government and its strong tradition of independence.

New Hampshire was the ninth state to join the Union. It officially joined on June 21, 1788.

New Hampshire is located in the New England region of the northeastern United States. It is bordered by Maine, Massachusetts, Vermont, and it also shares a short northern border with Canada.

Concord is the capital of New Hampshire. It officially became the capital in 1808.

Concord, New Hampshire, has an estimated population of about 43,900 people.

New Hampshire is the forty-sixth largest state in the United States by area.

46th

North Conway, New Hampshire

There are approximately 1,409,000 people residing in the state of New Hampshire.

Manchester, New Hampshire

Franklin Pierce was born on November 23, 1804, in the small town of Hillsborough, New Hampshire. He grew up surrounded by forests, farms, and the quiet beauty of New England. Pierce worked hard in school, became a lawyer, and eventually served as the 14th President of the United States.

New Hampshire is known for its fresh apple cider donuts, especially in the fall. These warm, cinnamon-sugar treats are made with real apple cider from local orchards, giving them a cozy, sweet flavor. Families often enjoy them after apple-picking or at autumn festivals, making them one of the state's most beloved seasonal foods.

NEW HAMPSHIRE

There are 10 counties in New Hampshire.

Here is a list of those counties:

Belknap
Carroll
Cheshire
Coös
Grafton
Hillsborough
Merrimack
Rockingham
Strafford
Sullivan

Flume Gorge is one of New Hampshire's most magical places to explore. This natural granite passageway sits at the base of Mount Liberty in Franconia Notch State Park, where towering rock walls rise nearly 90 feet above your head. The easy, two-mile loop trail leads families across wooden boardwalks, past sparkling waterfalls, and through narrow pathways carved by rushing water thousands of years ago.

Funspot in Laconia is officially recognized as the largest arcade in the world. It opened in 1952 and has grown to include more than 600 games, including classic arcade machines, pinball, and candlepin bowling. Families visit from all over the country to experience this New Hampshire landmark.

The Cornish–Windsor Covered Bridge connects Cornish, New Hampshire, with Windsor, Vermont, across the Connecticut River. It is one of the longest wooden covered bridges in the United States, stretching 449 feet. Built in 1866, the bridge uses a special lattice-truss design that helps support its long span. It remains an important historic landmark and a classic example of New England covered-bridge engineering.

The New Hampshire state bird is the Purple Finch. It was chosen as the state bird in 1957.

The official state flower of New Hampshire is the Purple Lilac. It was chosen as the state flower in 1919.

A couple of New Hampshire's nicknames include the Granite State and the White Mountain State.

ST8

ST8

New Hampshire's state motto is "Live Free or Die." It became the official state motto in 1945.

LIVE

FREE

The abbreviation for New Hampshire is NH.

NH

New Hampshire's state flag was officially adopted in 1909.

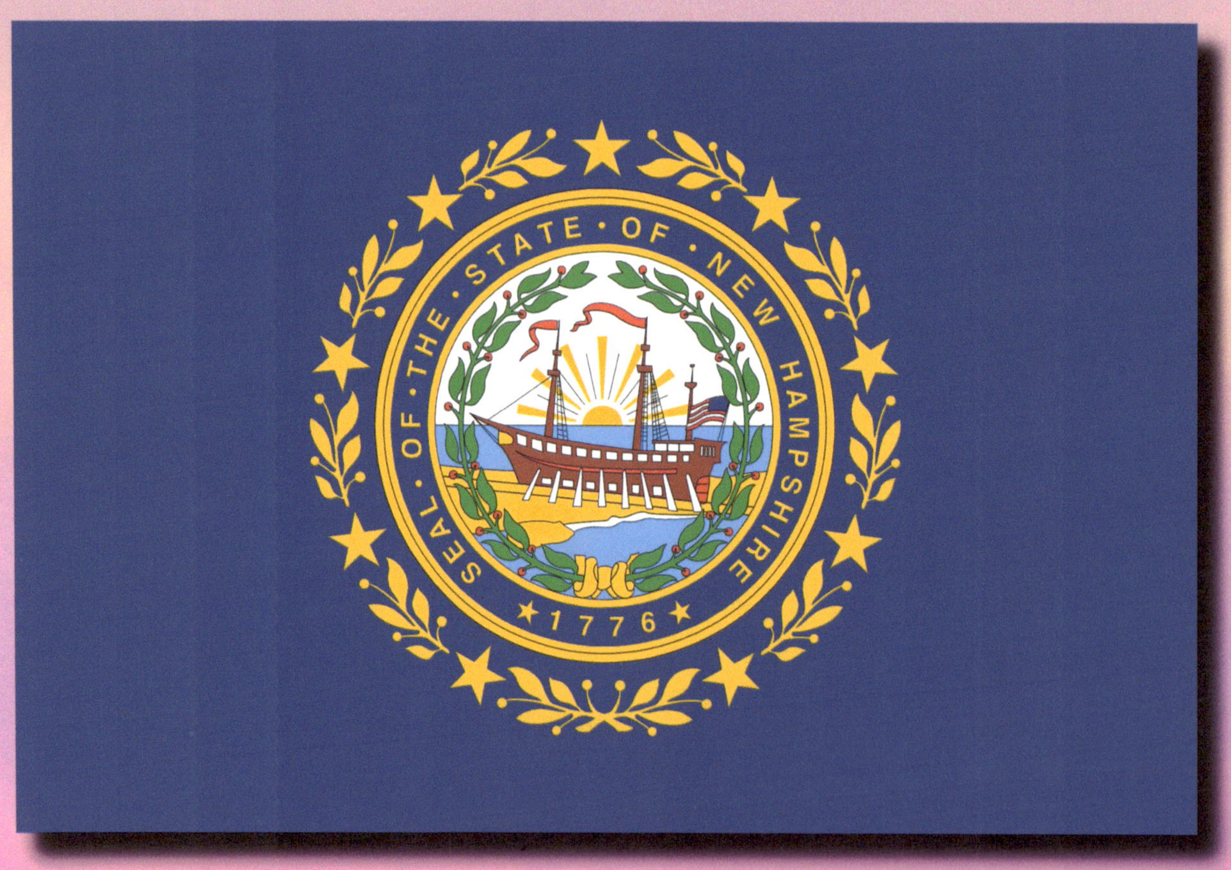

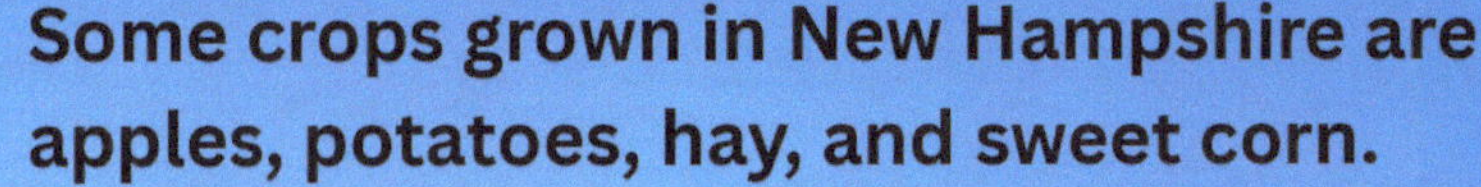

Some crops grown in New Hampshire are apples, potatoes, hay, and sweet corn.

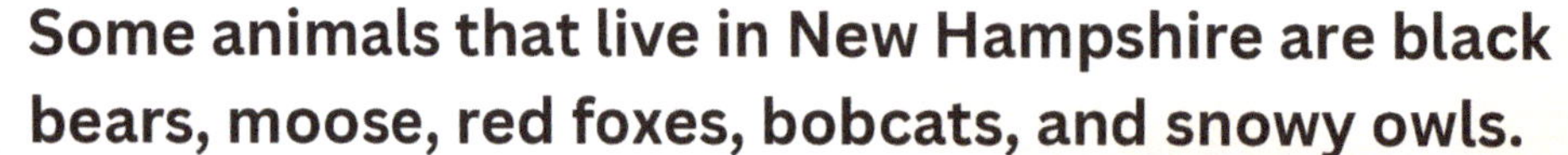

Some animals that live in New Hampshire are black bears, moose, red foxes, bobcats, and snowy owls.

New Hampshire experiences a wide range of temperatures throughout the year. The hottest temperature ever recorded in the state was 106 degrees Fahrenheit, measured in Nashua on July 4, 1911. In contrast, the coldest temperature documented was −50 degrees Fahrenheit, recorded on Mount Washington on January 22, 1885.

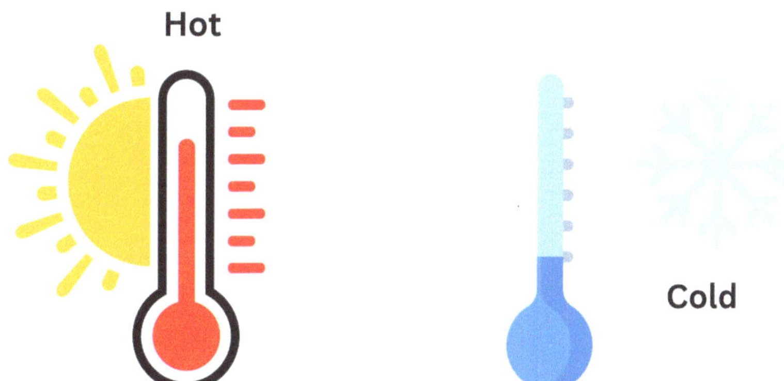

The Squam Lakes Natural Science Center in Holderness, New Hampshire, is a wonderful place where kids can learn about animals that live in the region. Families can see black bears, river otters, mountain lions, owls, and other native wildlife while exploring outdoor trails and nature exhibits.

Franconia Notch State Park is one of New Hampshire's most breathtaking places, where rugged mountains, quiet forests, and sparkling lakes all come together in one stunning landscape. Families can explore rocky paths, peaceful ponds, and miles of scenic trails.

The largest airport in New Hampshire is Manchester–Boston Regional Airport, located in Manchester, in the southern part of the state. It sits at 1 Airport Road, Manchester, New Hampshire, and serves as the main travel hub for people flying in and out of New Hampshire. The airport connects travelers to cities across the country and is known for its easy layout, friendly atmosphere, and welcoming New England feel.

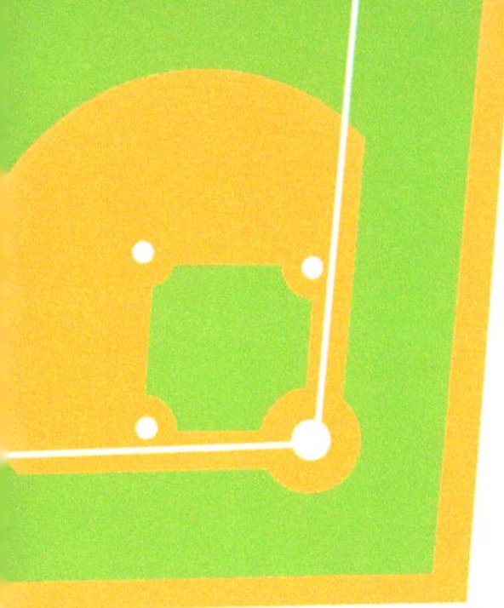

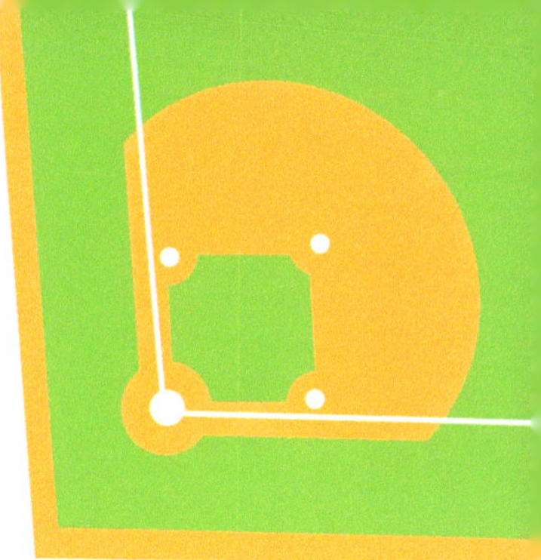

The New Hampshire Fisher Cats are a Minor League Baseball team based in Manchester, right along the Merrimack River. They play their home games at Delta Dental Stadium, a cheerful ballpark known for its family-friendly atmosphere and beautiful views of the river and city skyline.

FOOTBALL

The University of New Hampshire Wildcats are the most well-known football team in the state, and they play in Durham, in the southeastern part of New Hampshire. Their home field is Wildcat Stadium, a lively place where fans bundle up in blue and white to cheer on the team. The Wildcats are known for their tough, energetic play and the strong sense of community that fills the stadium on game days, making each matchup feel like a true New Hampshire tradition.

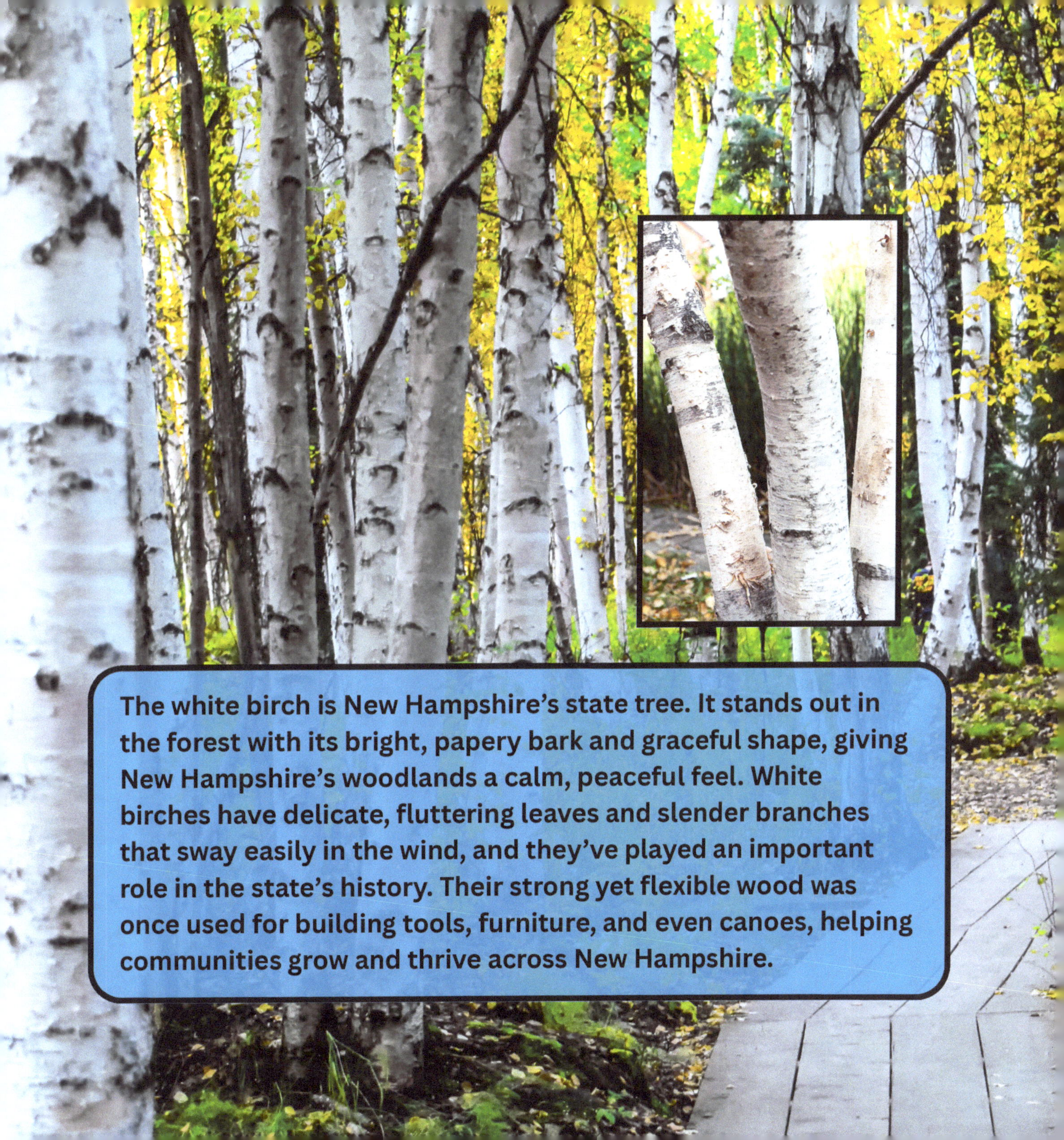

The white birch is New Hampshire's state tree. It stands out in the forest with its bright, papery bark and graceful shape, giving New Hampshire's woodlands a calm, peaceful feel. White birches have delicate, fluttering leaves and slender branches that sway easily in the wind, and they've played an important role in the state's history. Their strong yet flexible wood was once used for building tools, furniture, and even canoes, helping communities grow and thrive across New Hampshire.

The brook trout is New Hampshire's state fish. It's a colorful, speckled fish known for its quick swimming and graceful movements as it glides through New Hampshire's cold, clear streams and mountain ponds. Even though it's strong and lively, the brook trout is a calm creature, spending most of its time weaving through cool waters in search of insects and small aquatic creatures. Its bright colors and love of clean, wild places make it one of the most treasured fish.

Can you name these?

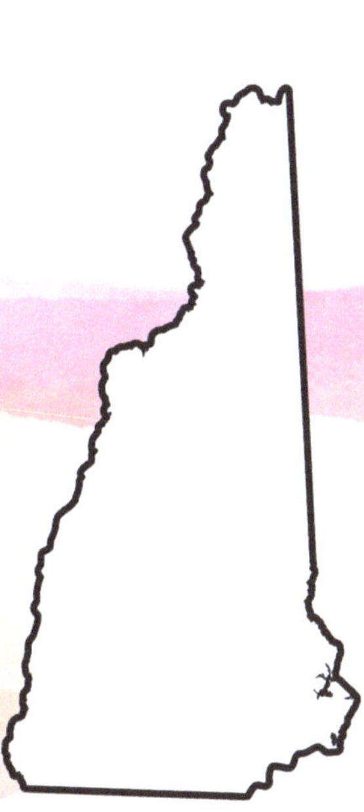

I hope you enjoyed learning about New Hampshire.

To explore fun facts about the other 49 states, visit my website at www.joeysavestheday.com. You'll also find a wide variety of homeschool resources to support joyful learning at home. If you enjoyed this book, I would be grateful if you left a review. Your feedback truly helps. Thank you for your support!

Check out these other interesting books in the 50 States Fact Books Series!

www.mimibooks.com

www.ingramcontent.com/pod-product-compliance
Lightning Source LLC
LaVergne TN
LVHW070201110826
845147LV00002B/461

* 9 7 8 1 9 5 8 9 8 5 8 5 4 *